Flowers in Tears

Flowers
in tears

Moniek Vanden Berghe

Photography: Kurt Dekeyzer

stichting
kunstboek

foreword

Arranging flowers for funerals has always been close to my heart. As a florist, one is in a special position to comfort the next of kin in their bereavement. By translating their gratefulness and love into an appropriate flower arrangement, one can help them give their loved one an unforgettable farewell.
I have always believed that flowers have the power to comfort people. Their refined energy is subtle yet prominent at a funeral, cremation or wake. One has to find the right flowers that best reflect the deceased and his/her loved ones.

Sadly, I found myself in this situation when my friend, Chris, whom I had known for 33 years, passed away. For this reason, I would like to dedicate this book to him. Chris was nearly 63 years when he passed away after a short, intense illness, on 10 April 2006. Ellen, his wife, and Lieve and Hendrieneke, his daughters, turned their farewell to him into a beautiful and moving event. The flower arrangements contributed to this dignified and poignant parting.

The book starts with the flower arrangements we made for Chris. During the evening of the farewell ceremony, we gave everyone a triangular piece of paper on which they wrote a message for Chris. Later on, I arranged all the notes in a large circle. The idea was to set it afloat during the scattering of his ashes on his birthday, 3 September.

On the left, the arrangement is airy and transparent, drawing the eye to the centre with the densely packed notes and Hellebores flowers to form Chris's favourite colour. The same colour was used in other arrangements placed at the farewell ceremony and later the cremation. Shortly before the cremation, everyone placed a handful of rose petals on his body. This moving image will stay with me forever. His body slowly disappeared under a blanket of petals. People using flowers to gently say good-bye to their loved one … painfully beautiful.

There are a great many symbolic ways of using flowers to say your farewells. Even if the florist did not know the deceased that well, one has to be open to the suggestions of the next of kin or the specific wishes of the deceased.
I am sure that making funeral flower arrangements for the closest loved ones can be one of the most meaningful assignments any florist could ever carry out. I am greatly inspired by this type of arrangement in my daily work. I hope that other florists will use this book as a source of inspiration to unlock their imagination.

Moniek Vanden Berghe

avant-propos

J'ai toujours accordé une attention particulière aux compositions funéraires. En tant que fleuriste, la chance unique nous est donnée d'assister les proches dans leur chagrin. En donnant forme à leur gratitude et à leur tendresse pour le défunt par un arrangement floral approprié, je peux les aider à prendre congé de l'être aimé d'une manière inoubliable. J'ai toujours eu le sentiment que les fleurs apportent une vraie consolation. Avec leur énergie raffinée, elles sont modestes tout en étant bien présentes lors de funérailles, d'une crémation ou d'une cérémonie d'adieu. Il ne doit pas s'agir d'une masse de fleurs, il faut trouver la note florale qui s'accorde à cette personne et à ses proches.

Hélas, j'en ai fait la triste expérience lorsque mon ami Chris s'en est allé après 33 ans d'amitié, bien trop tôt. Aussi est-ce à lui que je tiens à dédier ce livre. Chris n'avait que 63 ans lorsqu'il s'en est allé le 10 avril 2006, après une maladie brève et aigüe. Ellen, sa femme, et Lieve et Hendrieneke, ses filles, en ont fait des adieux pleins de beauté et d'émotion. Par le biais de nos fleurs, nous aussi avons pu faire de dignes adieux.

Le livre s'ouvre dès lors par les compositions que nous avons réalisées pour lui. Avant la soirée d'adieu, nous avions fabriqué des billets triangulaires sur lesquels toutes les personnes présentes pouvaient noter leur message à l'intention de Chris. Par la suite, j'ai intégré tous ces messages dans une grande composition circulaire. L'objectif était de le mettre à l'eau, près du lieu de la dispersion des cendres, le 3 septembre, le jour de l'anniversaire de Chris.

A gauche, la composition est aérienne et transparente, toute l'attention est attirée vers le centre, où les messages et les fleurs d'hellébores se concentrent jusqu'au plan dans la couleur favorite de Chris. La même couleur revient aussi dans les autres compositions agencées à ses côtés au moment de la cérémonie et lors de la crémation. Dans les instants précédant la crémation, nous avons tous déposé une poignée de pétales de roses sur le corps de Chris. Cette image émouvante m'a marquée à jamais... Lentement, Chris a été recouvert d'une tendre couverture de fleurs. Des hommes et des fleurs en mouvement autour d'un être aimé en partance, un moment à la fois douloureux et beau.

D'innombrables gestes floraux symboliques peuvent être posés lors d'un adieu. Même lorsque le fleuriste n'a pas très bien connu la personne décédée, il doit être ouvert aux souhaits spécifiques de ses proches ou des préférences exprimées naguère par le défunt même. Je suis convaincue que la réalisation de pièces florales funéraires, et surtout si on les réalise pour les êtres les plus proches du défunt, représente l'une des missions les plus sensées qu'un fleuriste puisse accomplir. Pour moi, il s'agit en tous cas d'une partie inspirante de notre travail quotidien. Que ce livre soit pour de nombreux fleuristes une source nouvelle et chaleureuse d'inspiration.

Moniek Vanden Berghe

voorwoord

Aan het maken van rouwbloemwerk heb ik altijd al heel veel aandacht besteed. Als florist krijg je een heel bijzondere en mooie kans om nabestaanden bij te staan in hun verdriet. Door hun dankbaarheid en tederheid voor de overledene in een passend bloemenarrangement vorm te geven, kan je hen helpen om de geliefde een onvergetelijk afscheid te bezorgen.

Ik heb altijd het gevoel gehad dat bloemen echt troosten. Met hun verfijnde energie zijn ze bescheiden maar toch uitdrukkelijk aanwezig bij een uitvaart, crematie of begroeting. Het hoeft allerminst om een bloemenzee te gaan. Je moet de juiste bloemengroet vinden die net zo goed past bij deze persoon en zijn geliefden.

Ik heb het helaas zelf in de realiteit meegemaakt toen ik mijn vriend Chris na 33 jaar vriendschap — te vroeg — verloor. Dit boek wil ik dan ook graag aan hem opdragen. Chris was amper 63 jaar toen we hem na een korte, hevige ziekte moesten loslaten op 10 april 2006. Ellen, zijn vrouw, en Lieve en Hendrieneke, zijn dochters, hebben er een mooi en aangrijpend afscheid van gemaakt. Via onze bloemen hebben ook wij hem een waardig vaarwel kunnen zeggen.

Het boek begint dan ook met de composities die we voor hem maakten. Voor de avond van de afscheidsbijeenkomst hadden we driehoekige briefjes gemaakt waarop alle aanwezigen hun boodschap voor Chris konden neerschrijven. Later heb ik alle boodschappen verwerkt in een grote cirkelcompositie. Het was de bedoeling om die op 3 september, Chris' verjaardag, mee te geven op het water bij de asverstrooiing.

Links is de compositie luchtig en transparant, alle aandacht richt zich naar het centrum waar boodschappen en Helleborusbloemetjes zich samen verdichten tot bij het vlak in de favoriete kleur van Chris. Dezelfde kleur werd ook gebruikt in de andere composities naast hem op het moment van de ceremonie en bij de crematiebijeenkomst.

Vlak voor de crematie hebben we met z'n allen een handjevol rozenblaadjes neergelegd op het lichaam van Chris. Dit ontroerende beeld zal me altijd bijblijven ... Hoe hij langzaam onder een groeiend en teder bloemendeken kwam te liggen. Mensen en bloemen in beweging rond de geliefde die heenging, pijnlijk mooi.

Er zijn werkelijk talloze mooie symbolische bloemengebaren te maken bij een afscheid. Ook als je als florist de overledene minder goed kent, moet je je openstellen voor de specifieke wensen van de nabestaanden of de uitdrukkelijke voorkeur van de overledene zelf. Ik ben er zeker van dat rouwbloemwerk, zeker als je het maakt voor de dichtste geliefden van de overledene, een van de meest zinnige opdrachten is die je als florist kunt volbrengen. Voor mij is het alvast een inspirerend onderdeel van ons dagelijks werk. Ik hoop dat veel floristen in dit boek nieuwe en warme inspiratie mogen vinden.

Moniek Vanden Berghe

Flowers   'extend their loving arms'
          symbolizing the deep bond
          between togetherness and separation

I met her on a day like any other.
Her presence left an impression on me ... light like a dandelion clock.
Unobtrusive, rather cautious and attentive, her presence was
tangible. Sometimes even reserved, like a shadow. Other times,
very intense, yet delicate like a forget-me-not.

On a day like any other, death announced itself in my life.
Unexpectedly. Life came to a standstill — it had lost its meaning.
Words meant nothing.
Only bewilderment and inhuman sorrow were left.
How do you say the unsayable?
How can you speak of the past while sorrow drowns your words?

She knew.
Moniek knew before me.

With her unmistakable refinement, her sense of dignity and
warmth, she knew that flowers could express feelings as others did
with words:

'Let my sorrow be greater than yours
to embrace it like arms' *

Her flowers expressed my deepest feelings: tenderly they em-
braced my sorrow with love.
Thank you, Moniek, for every shared moment, for the privilege of
your talent, for your artistic soul, but, especially, just for being you.

Annemie Claeys-Van Rossen

* Herman de Coninck

Dear Moniek and Ward,

When I met Chris eight years ago, he talked about the people in
his life who meant a lot to him. I realized straightaway that your
friendship meant the world to him.

It took a while before I had the pleasure of meeting you, and
the wonderful creations you make.
'When we get married, I'm going to ask Moniek to create a
bouquet for you', Chris told me in the early days. And he kept
his promise: your creations surpassed all my expectations. Your
flower arrangements added magic to our most beautiful day.

A few weeks later, Chris passed away ... And yet again your
flowers captured the spirit of the day. A final embrace with
flowers, reflecting our unspoken feelings. I had never seen
anything so beautiful.

Chris's death has left us heartbroken. But, at the same time,
the way we experienced his last moments and the lasting
impression he left are a source of inspiration for us who stay
behind. The same inspiration brought about this book. Thank
you for dedicating this book to him. I hope the photos will fill
the readers with beauty and strength in times of sorrow.

All my love
Ellen

Des fleurs 'comme des bras'
	comme un lien étroit entre
	l'union et la séparation

Je l'ai rencontrée un jour comme tous les autres.
Elle laissait des traces, légères et attachantes, comme celles d'un plumeau de pissenlit. Non qu'elle s'imposait, au contraire : elle était toujours présente, attentionnée et prudente.
Tantôt réservée, comme une ombre. Tantôt très intense, avec la délicate pureté d'un myosotis.

Un jour comme tous les autres, la mort est entrée dans ma vie, inopinément.
Tout s'est arrêté, plus rien n'avait de sens. Il n'y avait plus de mots, plus de beauté, rien que la stupeur et un chagrin inhumain.
Comment exprimer ce qui ne peut l'être ?
Comment parler de ce qui était alors que le chagrin vous frappe de stupeur ?

Elle le savait.
Moniek le savait avant moi.

Avec ce raffinement subtil qui lui est propre, avec son sens du respect,
sa chaleur intérieure, elle savait qu'elle en était capable : exprimer avec des fleurs ce qu'un autre grand artiste a fait avant elle avec des mots :

*'Laisse mon chagrin être toujours plus grand que le tien
Pour qu'il puisse l'étreindre comme des bras'* *

Ses fleurs disaient ce que je ressentais dans chacune de mes fibres,
avec une douceur apaisante, elle leur faisait faire ce que je ne pouvais plus donner : une étreinte d'amour et de consolation.
Merci, Moniek, pour tous les moments d'émotion partagée, pour l'expérience de ton grand talent, pour la force de ton âme d'artiste,
pour ces valeurs très particulières que tu portes en toi.

Annemie Claeys-Van Rossen

* Herman de Coninck

Chers Moniek et Ward,

Lorsque j'ai rencontré Chris il y a huit ans, il m'a parlé de toutes les personnes qu'il portait dans s on cœur. D'emblée, j'ai réalisé combien votre amitié comptait pour lui.

Il s'est écoulé du temps avant que je puisse vous rencontrer à mon tour, et lorsque j'ai fait votre connaissance, j'ai aussi découvert vos superbes réalisations.

'Lorsque nous nous marierons', me disait Chris, 'je demande-rai à Moniek de te réaliser un bouquet de mariée'. Lorsque ce jour est arrivé, la composition que tu avais réalisée a dépassé toutes mes espérances. Et telles une multitude de cerises sur le gâteau, tes décorations florales ont donné encore plus de lustre à cette superbe journée.

Quelques semaines plus tard, Chris nous a quittés …
Et une fois de plus, ce sont tes fleurs, vos fleurs, qui sont venues encadrer l'atmosphère de ce moment. Une dernière étreinte que les fleurs ont pu donner lorsque nous, humains, ne pouvions plus le faire ; c'étaient les plus belles fleurs que j'aie jamais vues.

La disparition de Chris était et est toujours un grand chagrin.
En même temps, la manière dont nous avons vécu ses derniers moments ensemble et l'impression qu'il a laissée sont une source d'inspiration constante pour le reste de nos jours. C'est cette même inspiration qui a permis la réalisation de ce livre. Aussi suis-je très heureuse que vous lui dédiez cet ouvrage et j'espère que les photos qu'il contient apporteront à nombre de lecteurs beauté et force de vie dans les moments de chagrin.

*Avec toute mon affection,
Ellen*

Bloemen 'als armen'
    als innige band tussen
    samen zijn en scheiden

Ik ontmoette haar op een dag als alle andere.
Zij liet sporen na, licht en beklijvend als die van een paardenbloempluis.
Niet dat ze zich opdrong, integendeel, steeds behoedzaam en attent
bleef ze aanwezig. Gereserveerd soms, als een schaduw. Dan weer heel
intens met de delicate puurheid van een vergeet-mij-niet.

Op een dag als alle andere kwam de dood in mijn leven, heel onverwacht.
Alles stond stil, niets had verder zin.
Er waren geen woorden meer, geen schoonheid, enkel verbijstering en
onmenselijk verdriet.

Hoe uitdrukken wat niet uit te drukken valt.
Hoe spreken over wat was terwijl verdriet je met verstomming slaat.

Zij wist het.
Moniek wist het voor mij.

Met subtiele verfijning, haar zo eigen, met haar zin voor respect,
haar innerlijke warmte, wist zij dat het kon: met bloemen uitdrukken
wat een ander groot kunstenaar haar voordeed met woorden:

'Laat mijn verdriet altijd groter wezen dan het jouwe
Zodat het eromheen kan liggen als armen'*

Haar bloemen zegden wat ik in elke vezel voelde, met zachte zorg liet zij
hen overnemen wat ik niet meer kon: troostend liefdevol omarmen.

Dank je Moniek voor elk moment van ontroering samen, voor het ervaren
van je grote talent, voor de kracht van je kunstzinnige ziel, voor dat heel
bijzondere in jou.

Annemie Claeys-Van Rossen

        * Herman de Coninck

Lieve Moniek en Ward,

Toen Chris en ik elkaar acht jaar geleden leerden kennen,
vertelde hij mij over alle mensen die hem na aan het hart
lagen. Het werd mij meteen duidelijk dat jullie vriendschap
heel belangrijk was voor hem.

Het duurde nog een tijdje voordat ook ik jullie kon ontmoeten,
en toen maakte ik niet alleen kennis met jullie, maar ook met
jullie prachtige werk.

'Als we gaan trouwen', zei Chris altijd tegen mij, 'vraag ik
Moniek om een bruidswerk voor je te maken'. Toen het
uiteindelijk zo ver was, overtrof wat je maakte al mijn
verwachtingen. En als kersjes op de taart maakten jouw
bloemenversieringen onze prachtige dag nog mooier.

Een paar weken later overleed Chris ...
En weer waren het jouw bloemen, júllie bloemen, die de
sfeer van dat moment omlijstten. Een laatste omhelzing die
de bloemen konden geven waar dat voor ons mensen niet
meer mogelijk was; het waren de mooiste bloemen die ik
ooit heb gezien.

De dood van Chris was en is een groot verdriet. Tegelijkertijd
zijn de manier waarop wij samen zijn levenseinde hebben
beleefd en de indruk die hij achterlaat een inspiratie voor de
rest van het leven. Het is dezelfde inspiratie die dit boek
mogelijk heeft gemaakt. Het maakt mij dan ook heel gelukkig
dat jullie dit boek aan hem opdragen. Ik hoop dat de foto's
vele lezers zullen vullen met schoonheid en levenskracht in
tijden van verdriet.

Met heel veel liefde,
Ellen

For Chris

Tulipa 'Black Parrot'
Helleborus x hybridus
Viburnum opulus 'Roseum'
Rosa 'Avant Garde'

Rosa 'Maroussia!'
Rosa 'Finesse'
Rosa 'Peach Avalanche'
Pyracantha coccinea
Asclepias curassavica
Passiflora aurentea

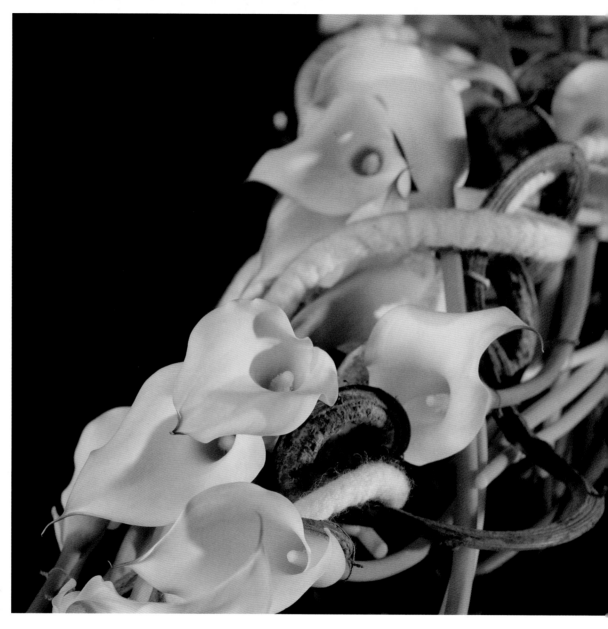

Zantedeschia 'Chrystal Blush'
Liane

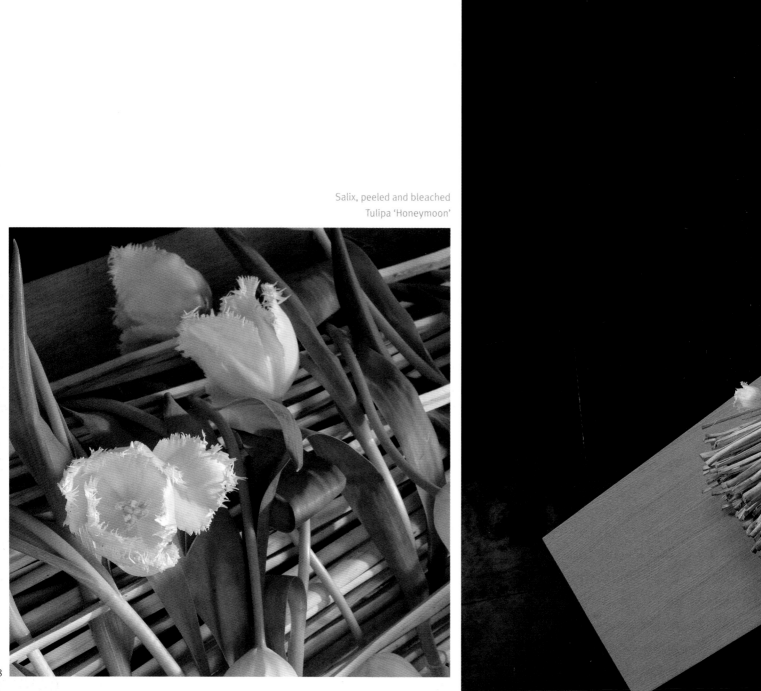

Salix, peeled and bleached
Tulipa 'Honeymoon'

18

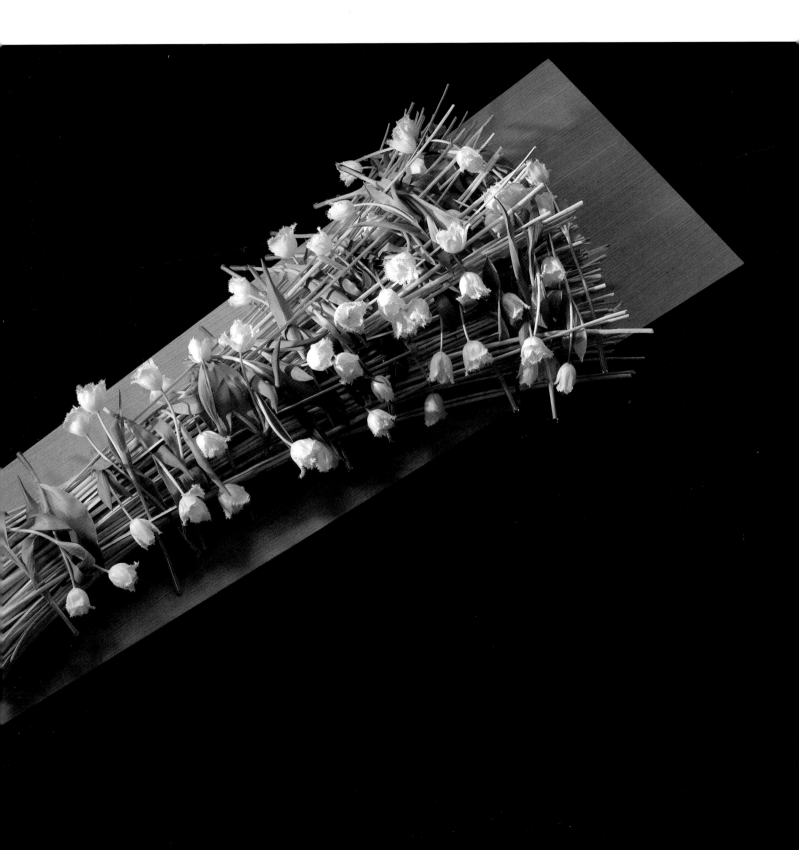

Bromus sterilis
Clematis 'Pirouette'
Wisteria floribunda
Hydrangea macrophylla
Nigella damascena
Dianthus caryophyllus
Eustoma grandiflorum 'Mysty blue'

Lilium longiflorum
Hydrangea macrophylla 'Schneeball'
Chrysanthemum 'Boris Becker'
Chrysanthemum (santini) 'Noki'
Prunus laurocerasus
Bromus sterilis

23

Hydrangea macrophylla 'Schneeball'
Vanda 'Pink Magic'
Calamus rotang (rattan palm)

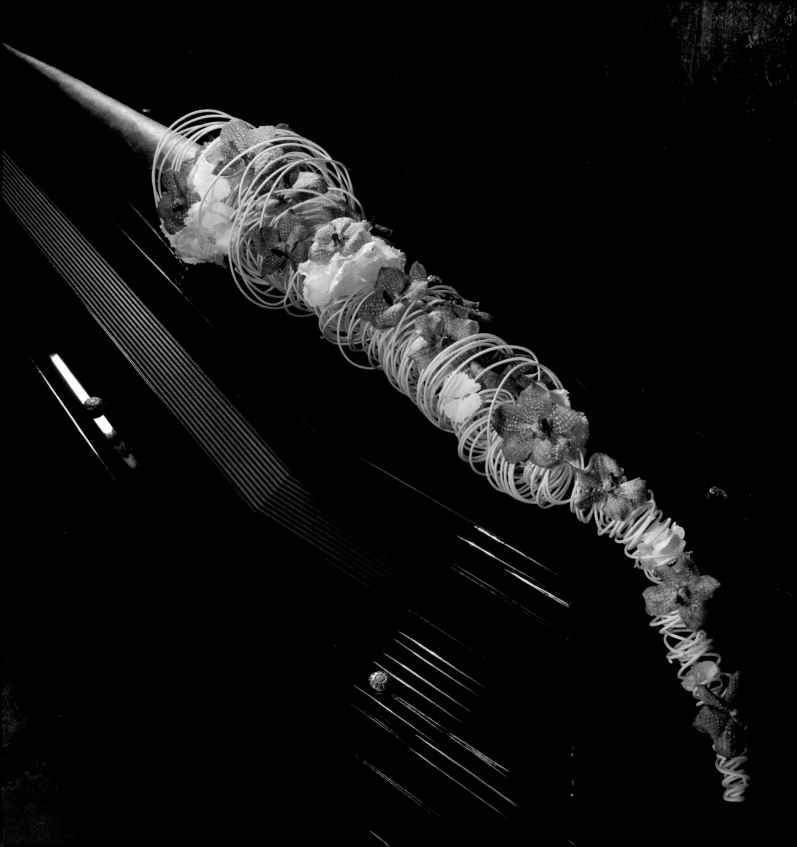

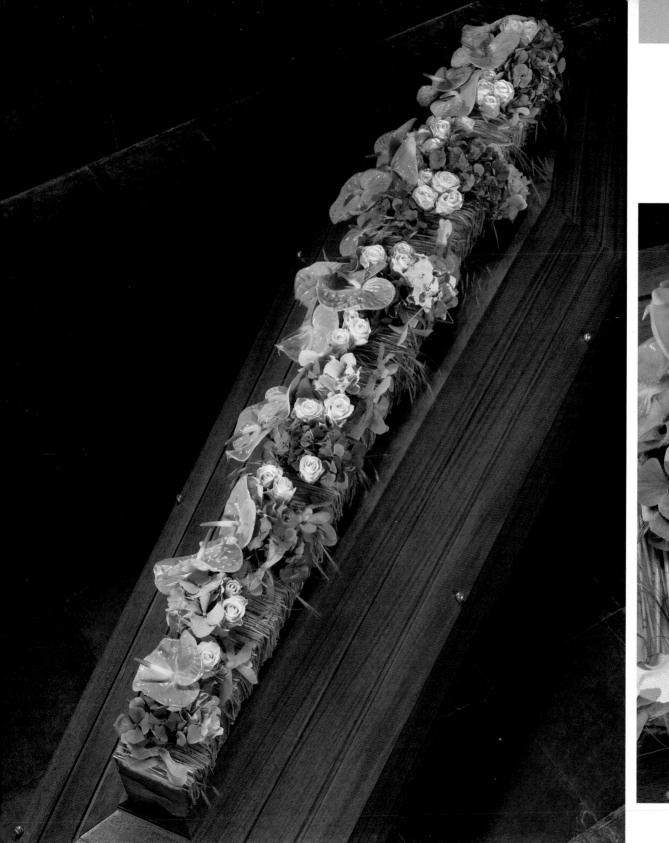

Anthurium 'Midori'
Hydrangea macrophylla
'Renate Steiniger'
Bromus sterilis
Rosa 'F Green'
Acer palmatum

Carex flagellifera
Alchemilla mollis
Paeonia 'Duchesse de Nemours'
Rosa 'F Green'

Phalaenopsis hybride
Sandersonia aurantiaca

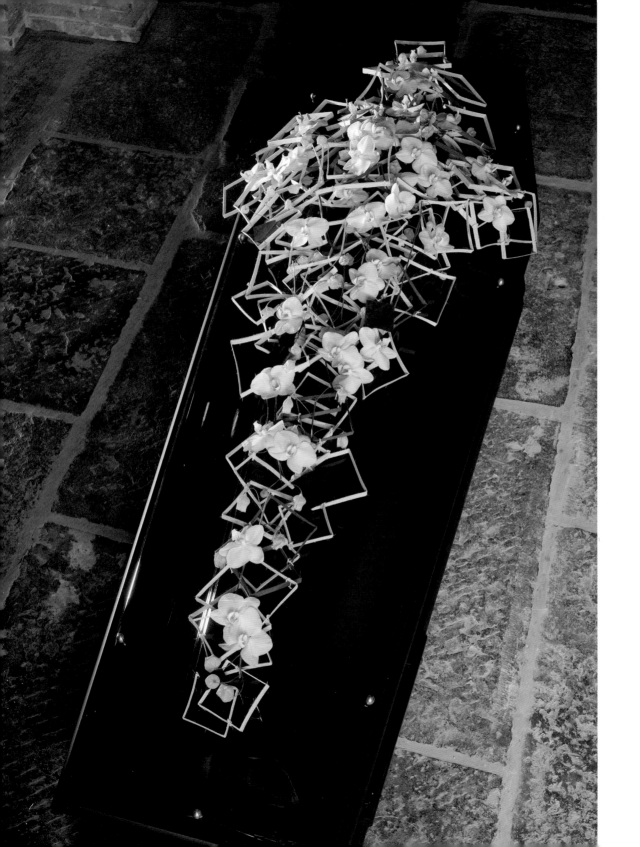

Rosa 'Marrousia!'
Hydrangea macrophylla
'Schneeball'
Cordyline australis

Bromus sterilis
Paeonia hybride
Spathiphyllum
Prunus laurocerasus

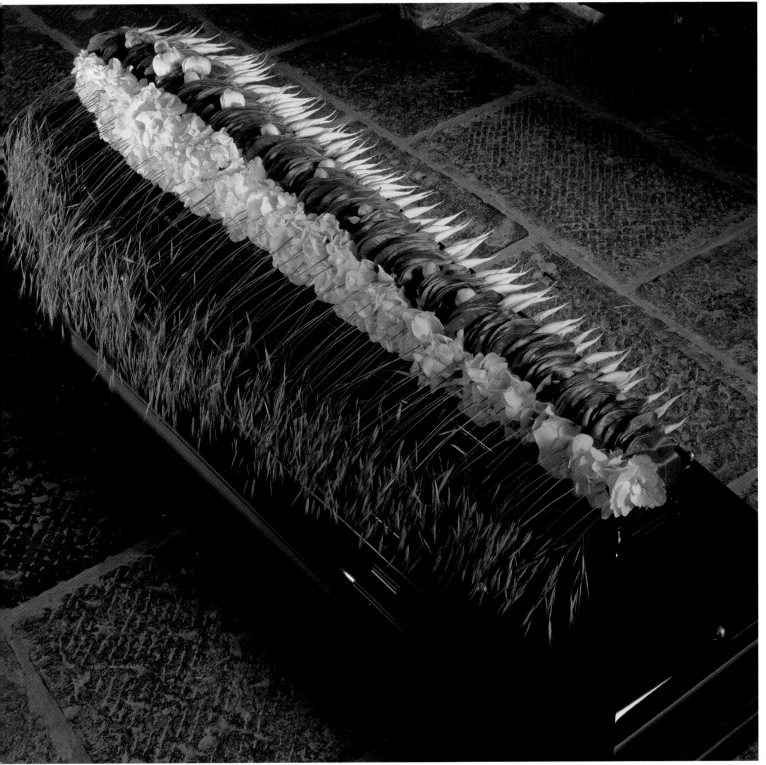

Begonia
Acer palmatum 'Dissectum Garnet'
Rosa 'Red Naomi!'
Taraxacum officinale
Hydrangea macrophylla 'Schneeball'
Miscanthus sinensis
Anthurium 'Maxima Elegance'

Mysosotis sylvaticum
Xerophyllum tenax
Adianthum pedatum
Cordyline australis
Hydrangea macrophylla
Viburnum opulus 'Roseum'

Ranunculus asiaticus hybride
Hydrangea macrophylla
Hyacinthus hybride
Cordyline australis
Tillandsia xerographica

Eucharis x grandiflora
Cordyline australis

Phalaenopsis hybride
Sambucus nigra

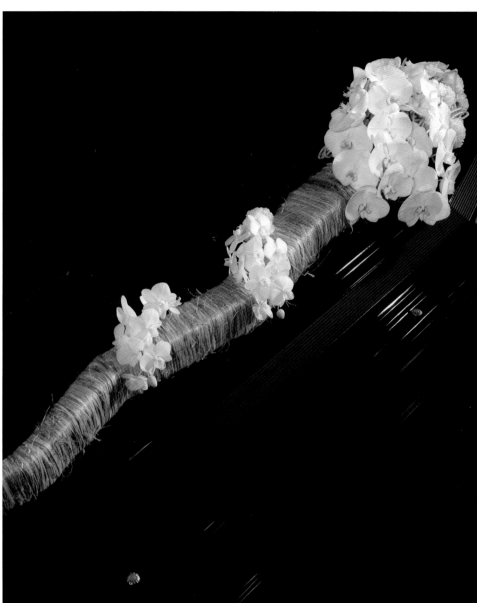

Phalaenopsis hybride
Dianthus caryophyllus

Rosa 'Avant Garde'
Hydrangea macrophylla
'Schneeball'
Clematis montana
Syringa vulgaris
Heuchera 'Palace Purple'
Anethum graveolens
'Purpurea'
Crambe maritima

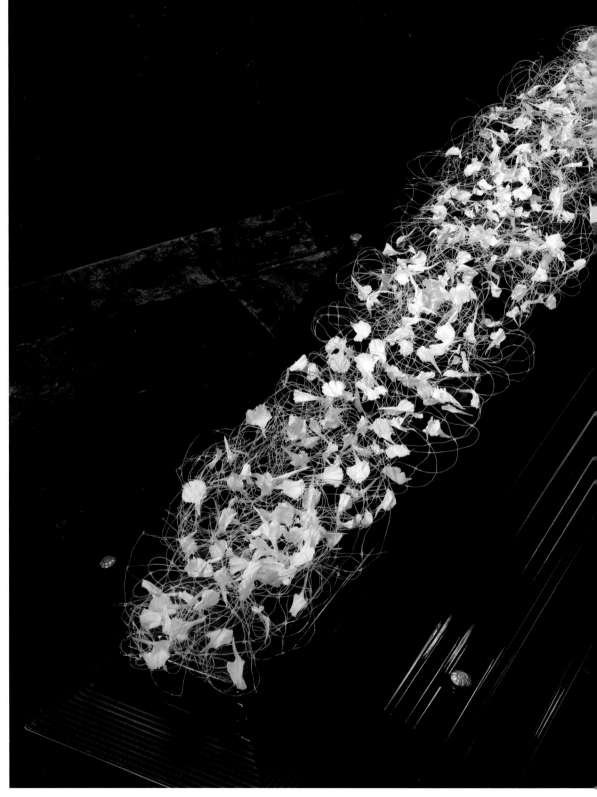

Dianthus caryophyllus

Eucharis x grandiflora
Liriope muscari 'Variegata'

Rosa 'Marrousia!'
Passiflora caerulea
Viccea cracca
Hydrangea macrophylla
Prunus lauricerasus

Rosa 'Marrousia!'
Bouvardia hybride
Hedera helix
Viburnum opulus 'Roseum'
Dracaena 'Lucky Bamboo'
Cordyline australis
Ranunculus asiaticus hybride

Rosa 'Marrousia!'
Bouvardia hybride
Hedera helix
Viburnum opulus 'Roseum'
Dracaena 'Lucky Bamboo'
Cordyline australis
Ranunculus asiaticus hybride

Kalanchoe bryophytum
scandens
Myosotis sylvatica

Vanda 'Dark Blue Magic'
Hydrangea macrophylla
Verbascum sp
Clematis vitalba

Sasa palmate
Rosa 'Supergreen'
Rosa 'Marroussia!'
Rosa 'Denise'
Ranunculua asiaticus hybride
Cordyline australis

Populus alba
Kalanchoe bryophytum
scandens
Ranunculus asiaticus hybride
Cordyline australis

Anthurium 'Snowy'
Bellis perennis
Asparagus asparagoides
Calamus rotang (rattan palm)
Rosa 'Sphinx Gold'
Physalis alkekengi
Dracaena sp

Rosa 'sphinx gold'
Physalis
Dracaena

Hippeastrum 'Swanlanke'
Salix, peeled and bleached
Senecio rowleyanus

Vanda 'Springtime Blue'
Hydrangea macrophylla
Tillandsia xerographica
Gleditsia triacanthos

Vanda 'Springtime Blue'
Aesculus hippocastaneum

Pahiopedilum
Asparagus asparagoides
Typha latifolia
Schinus molle

Hydrangea arborescens
Betula sp
Phalaenopsis hybride

Betula sp
Vanda 'Red Magic'
Clematis tangutica

Phalaenopsis 'Omega'
Rosa 'Amalia'
Rosa 'Silverstone'
Corylus maxima 'Purpurea'

Rosa 'Dreamlight'
Betula sp
Saxifraga

Populus alba
Ranunculus asiaticus hybride
Tillandsia xeropgraphica

Hedera helix
Ranunculus asiaticus hybride
Tillandsia xerographica

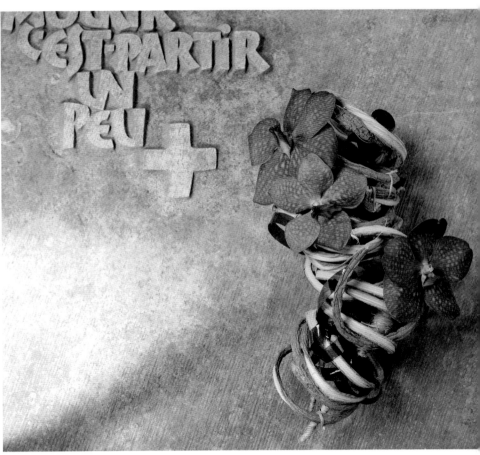

Vanda 'Cerise'
Liane

Rosa 'Piano'
Pernettya mucronata
Ligustrum
Cotinus coggygria 'Royal
Purple'

Indelible
intensive shared life
even short-lived
time was given.

Indelible
fragile and delicate existence
lives in our heart
as a precious pearl
and will accompany us always and everywhere.

Ineffaçable
partage intense de la vie
si bref que soit
le temps octroyé.

Ineffaçable
existence frêle et délicate
qui occupe notre coeur
et nous suivra en tout lieu et toute heure
telle une perle précieuse.

Onuitwisbaar
intens gedeeld leven
hoe kort ook
de tijd die werd gegeven.

Onuitwisbaar
breekbaar en broos bestaan
dat ons hart bewoont
en als een kostbare parel
overal en altijd met ons mee zal gaan.

Claire vanden Abbeele

Rosa 'Avant Garde'
Rosa 'Cool Water!'
Calocephalus brownii
Begonia Rex gr.
Ligustrum
Cordyline australis

73

Anthurium 'Midori'
Rosa 'F Green'
Bromus sterilis
Panicum virgatum
Cordyline australis
Dracaena vulgaris

Dianthus caryophyllus
Cordyline australis
Acer palmatum
Bromus sterilis

Nymphea
Rosa 'Ilios'
Hydrangea macrophylla
'Schneeball'
Taraxacum officinale
Salix, peeled and bleached
Pandanus latifolius

Elaeagnus x ebbingei
Platanus
Vanda hybride
Pittosporum 'Tobira'

Hibiscus syriacus
Corylus maxima 'Purpurea'
Vanda 'Red Magic'

Vanda 'Violet Red Magic'
Cotinus coggygria
Ligustrum
Pernettya mucronata
Raphia farinifera

Chrysanthemum 'Armgard'
Rosa 'Vendela'
Rosa 'Avant Garde'
Rosa 'Cool Water!'
Pandanus latifolius

Chrysanthemum 'Spider cuivre'
Zantedeschia

Zantedeschia 'Black Eyed Beauty'
Ginkgo biloba
Cotinus coggygria 'Royal Purple'

Vicea cracca
Prunus laurocerasus
Bouvardia longiflorum
Vanda 'Dark Blue Magic'
Vanda 'Blue Magic'

Cordyline australis
Chrysanthemum (santini) 'Froggy'
Hydrangea macrophylla 'Ayesha'
Dianthus 'Matriouska'

Anthurium 'Maxima Elegance'
Veneer wood
Rosa 'Grand Prix'
Rosa 'Tamango'
Cordyline australis

Anthurium 'P Alexia'
Hibiscus syriacus
Rosa 'Red Naomi!'
Morus alba

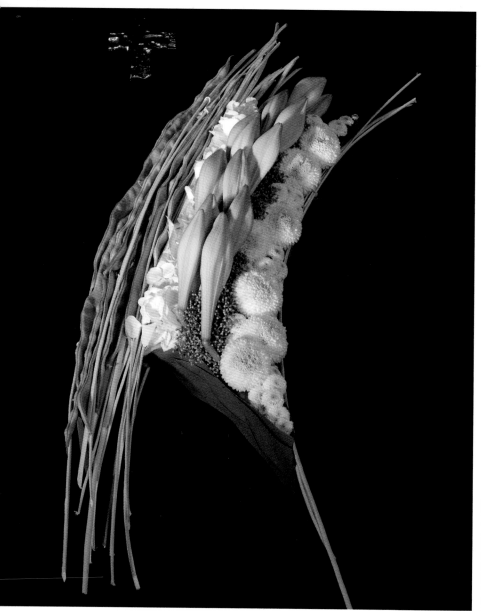

Lilium longiflorum
Cordyline australis
Skimmia japonica
Crysanthemum 'Boris Becker'
Chrysanthemum (santini) 'Noki'
Phaseolus vulgaris
Hydrangea macrophylla 'Schneeball'

Betula sp
Rosa 'Maroussia!'
Anthurium 'Midori'
Dianthus caryophyllus
Chrysanthemum 'Boris Becker'
Chrysanthemum (santini) 'Noki' and 'Froggy'

‹
Rosa 'F Green'
Chrysanthemum 'Balloon'
Asclepias tuberose
Clematis vitalba
Salix

‹‹
Anthurium 'Midori'
Skimmia japonica
Rosa 'F Green'
Chrysanthemum 'Balloon'
Chrysanthemum (santini) 'Froggy'
Cordyline australis
Ligustrum
Aristolochia

Syringa vulgaris
Clematis Montana
Rosa 'Avant Garde'
Dianthus caryophyllus
Trachelium
Rhoicissus
Pandanus

Anthurium 'Grace'
Salix
Lithops
Rosa 'Avant Garde'
Chrysanthemum (santini)

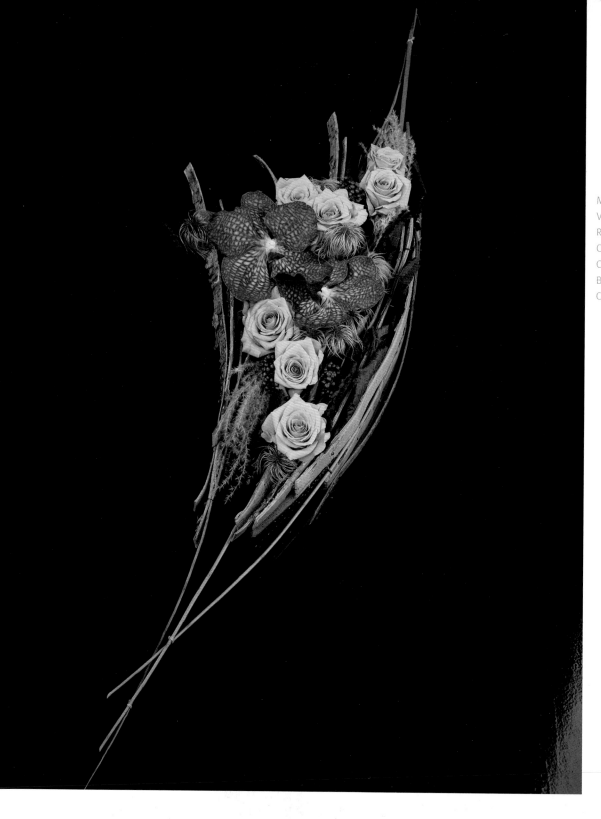

Miscanthus sinensis
Vanda 'Blue Magic'
Rosa 'Avant Garde'
Clematis tangutica
Callicarpa bodinieri
Betula sp
Corylus maxima 'Purpurea'

›

Vanda 'Cerise'
Hydrangea arborescens
Clematis vitalba
Betula sp
Cordyline australis

Gleditsia triacanthos
Vanda 'Black Magic'
Clematis vitalba
Palm sheath

Corylus maxima 'Purpurea'
Dendrobium
Lonicera
Orchid
Cobaea
Symphoricarpos orbiculatus
Ozothamnus diosmifolius

Cymbidium 'Gold Fleece'
Chrysanthemum 'Orange Kiev'
Betula sp
Cordyline australis
Corylus maxima 'Purpurea'

Vanda
Skimmia japonica
Platanus
Pittosporum 'Tobira'
Salix
Clematis tangutica

Brassica oleracea convar
capitata var. rubra
Chrysanthemum 'Balloon'
Chrysanthemum (santini) 'Froggy'
Vanda 'Black Magic'
Ligustrum
Rosa 'F Green'
Cordyline australis

Rosa 'Maroussia!'
Cordyline australis
Chrysanthemum 'Fred Shoesmith'
Chrysanthemum 'Balloon'
Agapanthus
Aristea confusa
Echinops ritro
Symphoricarpos orbiculatus

Pandanus
Lilium longiflorum
Hydrangea macrophylla 'Schneeball'
Prunus laurocerasus
Chrysanthemum 'Boris Becker'
Chrysanthemum (santini) 'Froggy'
Chrysanthemum (santini) 'Noki'

Chrysanthemum 'Ice Queen'/'Minsk Green'

Circles in the water
pearls in watering eyes
future dreams
colors and rainbows.

Circles, round and open
peace and quiet
symbols with hope
of a new view.

Ronds dans l'eau
perles dans les yeux larmoyants
rêves d'avenir
couleurs et arc-en-ciel.

Cercles, ronds et ouverts
calme et équilibre
symboles qui nous font espérer
en des horizons nouveaux.

Kringen in het water
parels in tranende ogen
dromen voor later
kleuren en regenbogen.

Cirkels, rond en open
rust en evenwicht
symbolen die ons laten hopen
op een nieuw vergezicht.

Claire vanden Abbeele

Vanda 'Cerise'
Vanda 'Magic Red'
Vandaenopsis
Clematis tangutica
Chrysanthemum 'Orange Kiev'
Callicarpa bodinieri
Ligustrum
Palm sheath
Rosa 'Torrero'
Rosa 'Peppermint'
Rosa 'Grand Prix'

Betula sp
Rosa 'Grand Prix'
Rosa 'Torrero'
Photinia
Clematis tangutica

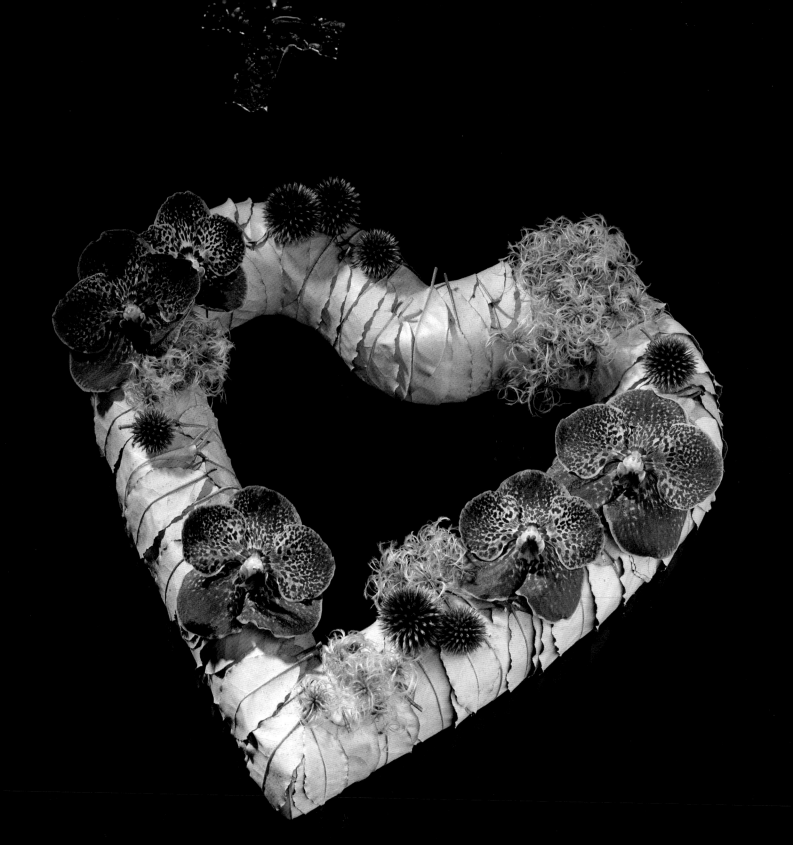

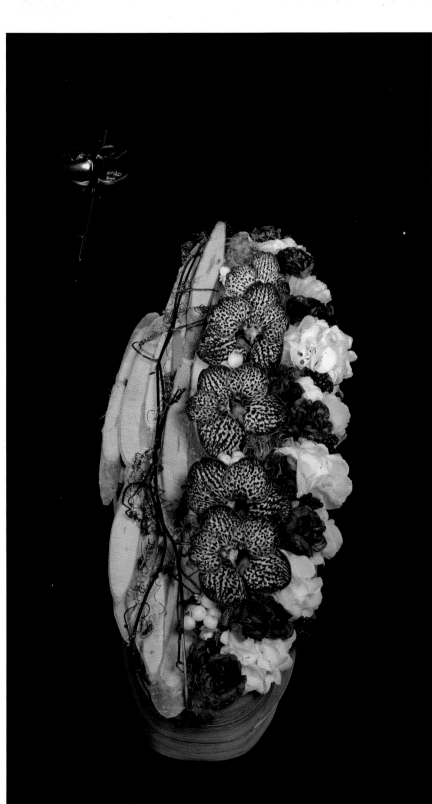

<
Vanda 'Black Magic'
Clematis vitalba
Eleagnus x ebbingei
Echinops ritro

<<
Vanda 'Exotic Purple'
Dianthus caryophyllus 'Neon Purple'
Hydrangea macrophylla 'Schneeball'
Populus
Cobaea
Clematis vitalba
Symphoricarpos orbiculatus

Clematis tangutica
Rosa 'King Arthur'
Pernettya mucronata
Cobaea
Betula sp

Duchesnea indica
Rubus fruticosus
Rosa 'Piano'
Gerbera (germini) 'Suri'
Dahlia 'red Cap'
Miscanthus sinensis
Cotinus coggygria
Cordyline australis

Medinilla
Viburnum opulus 'Roseum'
Rosa 'F Green'
Hydrangea 'Hovaria Hopalin'

Clematis Montana
Helleborus x hybridus
Trachelium
Cordyline australis
Sea urchins

Hydrangea macrophylla
Cimicifuga
Palm sheath
Pandanus
Dracaena
Anthurium 'Snowy'
Chrysanthemum 'Boris Becker'
Chrysanthemum (santini) 'Noki'

Salix
Pittosporum 'tobira'
Phalaenopsis
Clematis vitalba

117

A big thank-you

Kurt — For the beautiful exchange of ideas. You always find just the right angle, the perfect light. Working with you is always a pleasure.
Ward — For assisting me so well and for your technically creative ideas. Also for your involvement and full support for this project which meant so much to you.
Family — For your sincere interest and warm support.
Friends — What would I do without you?
Colleagues — Meeting you has been a source of inspiration.
My dear friends — Anne Marie and Ellen, for your heart-warming contributions.

Katrien Calsyn and Marc Van De Poele
Funerals, Sint-Laureins
For your much appreciated interest and cooperation.

Fantastic assistants:
Claire Caulier, Haruko Noda, Bart Van Didden, Trees and Sandy: my special angels

Also ...
Guy Herrel, because you are so close to my heart and still a positive influence in my life.
Thierry Smet, for your advice and information.
Harry van Trier, for your enormous botanical knowledge.
Frans Moens, Avalane, for the beautiful freeze-dried hellebores.
Henri Clijsters, Chris Martens and Jan Joris of Smithers Oasis,
for providing the necessary materials.
Steef van Adrichem, Anco, for the positive collaboration and the exquisite Vanda orchids.
Bjorn Mervilde and Kristof Musschoot, Godshuis Sint-Laureins, for the venue.
Family Hemschoote, Rekad Publishers, for the stimulating experience of Fleur Creatief.
Stichting Kunstboek, for the pleasant and professional collaboration.
Hugo Hendriks, Florever, for the compelling Flo-Art evenings.
Axel and Serge Vanden Bossche and the Serax team,
for your dynamic attitude and the freedom in our collaboration.
Claire vanden Abbeele, for your ever inspiring poetry.

Pieter Hein Boudens, epigraph, for your trust and the beautiful stone.
Ingrith Desmet, ceramic gallery, for the lovely urns.
Noelle De Vroey and Frank Lambert, for the permission to take pictures.
The flower suppliers, for their beautiful flowers, research and excellent service:
Gert Van Turnhout, Katty Proost and the team of the Agora group
Euroflor, the de Bleecker family
Dora Flora, Bart De Rijcke and assistants
Els Gennez, Chris Dimitriadis, Peter de Jaegher, Anne Denivel and Micha Vandormaal
for your great and easy collaboration.

Moniek Vanden Berghe

Training: floristry, IMOV, Gent.
Teacher Marc De Rudder
Demonstrations in Australia, Belgium,
France, Germany, Ireland, Japan, Korea,
the Netherlands, Scotland, UK, USA.

Kurt Dekeyzer

Photography at the VZH in Hasselt (laureate)
Founder of Photo Studio Graphics (PSG),
a full-service bureau with own photo
studio and design department.

Thank you, Chris, for 33 years of friendship and your inspirational presence in our life.

(Chris Maas 03.09.1942 – 10.04.2006)

Creations | Créations | Creaties
Moniek Vanden Berghe
Gravin Mad. d'Alcantaralaan 120
B-9971 Kaprijke (Lembeke)
T. +32 9 378 08 78
E. cleome@pandora.be
www.cleome.be

Photography | Photographies | Fotografie
Kurt Dekeyzer, PSG
Heidestraat 18
B-3470 Kortenaken
T. +32 11 22 09 95
E. kurt.dekeyzer@psg.be
www.psg.be

Ceramics: Catherine Vannier (p. 56), Delores Fortuna (p. 57),
Ursula Scheid (p. 58), Mieke Selleslagh (p. 59),
Sebastian Scheid (p. 60), Manous Halkiadakis (p. 61)

The works on the following pages were presented for the first time
on the demonstrations of Florever: p. 99, 116

Co-ordination | Coordination | Coördinatie
Karel Puype

Text | Textes | Tekst
Moniek Vanden Berghe
Ellen van der Velden
Annemie Claeys-Van Rossen
Claire vanden Abbeele (poems)

Final editing | Rédaction finale | Eindredactie
Eva Joos
Harry van Trier

English translation
Ilze Raath

Traduction française
Caroline Coppens

Layout & Print | Mise en pages & Impression | Vormgeving & Druk
Group Van Damme bvba, Oostkamp

Published by | Une édition de | Een uitgave van
Stichting Kunstboek bvba
Legeweg 165
B-8020 Oostkamp
T. +32 50 46 19 10
F. +32 50 46 19 18
E. info@stichtingkunstboek.com
www.stichtingkunstboek.com

ISBN 978-90-5856-268-5
D/2008/6407/6
NUR 421